PAUL DINI
MIKE BENSON
CHRIS YOST
Writers

DUSTIN NGUYEN
Penciller and Cover Artist

DEREK FRIDOLFS
Inker

JOHN KALISZ Colorist

SAL CIPRIANO STEVE WANDS JOHN J. HILL
Letterers

DUSTIN NGUYEN Original Series Cover Artist

BATMAN CREATED BY BOB KANE

# BATMAN STREETS OF GOTHAM LEVIATHAN

**Mike Marts**
Editor – Original Series

**Janelle Siegel**
Assistant Editor – Original Series

**Bob Harras**
Group Editor – Collected Editions

**Scott Nybakken**
Editor

**Robbin Brosterman**
Design Director – Books

**Curtis King Jr.**
Senior Art Director



**BATMAN: STREETS OF GOTHAM — LEVIATHAN**



DC Comics, 1700 Broadway
New York, NY 10019
A Warner Bros. Entertainment Company
Printed by RR Donnelley
Salem, VA. USA 9/30/11. First printing.

ISBN: 978-1-4012-2906-1

Fiber used in this product line meets the sourcing requirements of the SFI program. www.sfiprogram.org SGS-SFI/COC-US10/81072

TABLE OF CONTENTS

# BATMAN REBORN

In the aftermath of the universe-shattering events known as the Final Crisis, Gotham City's Dark Knight is presumed dead.

With the mantle of the Bat unclaimed, a battle erupts between Dick Grayson, the original Robin, and his corrupted successor, Jason Todd — just as the Black Mask destroys Arkham Asylum and sets its inmates loose to wreak havoc upon the vulnerable city.

In the resulting Battle for the Cowl, Dick Grayson is joined by Bruce Wayne's son Damian, and together they emerge victorious as a new and decidedly different Batman and Robin.

Meanwhile, after assuming the identity of Red Robin, former sidekick Tim Drake sets out on a quest that will eventually take him around the world — a quest to prove that the original Batman is still alive...

SAINT ALOYSIUS' CHURCH, GOTHAM CITY'S EAST END
SEVERAL YEARS AGO.
...CAN'T TELL YOU HOW THANKFUL I AM TO BE GIVEN THIS OPPORTUNITY. I LOOK FORWARD TO MEETING YOUR CONGREGATION HERE IN GOTHAM.
POP
UH-HUH.

YOU'VE SPENT OVER FORTY-FIVE YEARS HERE, FATHER MEL...I HOPE TO LEARN AS MUCH AS I CAN FROM YOU BEFORE YOU RETIRE NEXT MONTH...
UH-HUH.
I'M JUST SO EXCITED TO HAVE THE CHANCE TO ACTUALLY WORK IN A COMMUNITY THAT NEEDS ME, NOT LIKE IN METROPOLIS.

PFFT...SON...JUST STOP. JUST TELL ME ONE THING...
MARK, RIGHT? TELL ME, MARK... WHO DID YOU TICK OFF TO GET SENT TO THIS HELL HOLE?

MY FAITH BROUGHT ME HERE.
UH-HUH.
WELL, HERE'S MY ADVICE, BECAUSE I'M LEAVING TOMORROW. YOUR FAITH BROUGHT YOU HERE? THEN HOLD ON TO IT TIGHT.
THIS IS GOTHAM. IT'S NOT A CITY...IT'S A LEVIATHAN. YOUR FAITH WON'T BE TESTED HERE. HERE, THE BEAST HIMSELF WILL COME OUT AND RIP IT FROM YOU.
"IT'S NOT ENOUGH TO HAVE FAITH...YOU HAVE TO FIGHT TO KEEP IT IN GOTHAM."

NOW.
BATMAN
STREETS OF
GOTHAM

My name is Helena Bertinelli.
I call myself ***The Huntress.***

*Not so long ago, I swore that I would free Gotham City from the grip of the mob. That I would **save** Gotham.*

*If I had to make the same decision today? I think I'd choose to save someplace in the south of France. Marseilles, maybe.*

*Because for the most part? Gotham City can go to **hell.***

# LEVIATHAN

## PART 1 OF 2

The giant monster trying to kill me? Kirk Langstrom, the Man-Bat.
SHUNK
SHUNK
UHN!
Why's he trying to eat me? No idea.
I fire wide, just to avoid the lectures. Oracle and Nightwing...
Not Nightwing. Batman.
Batman would get all upset at me for killing him, and I'd never hear the end of it.
The irony is that Barbara told me that Langstrom was showing more self-control of late.
Supposedly he could even transform from man to Man-Bat and back again, without the serum he normally takes to initiate the change.
HT!
Well, Oracle needs to update her files, because "control" isn't on the menu today.
WHUMP
Yet another case of Batman giving a monster a second chance.
Jason Todd, Two-Face, Riddler...now this animal.
THAK
If there's a man left inside there, can't see it
Sometim with anima you have put ther down.

ut no. I don't get
to do the smart,
reasonable thing.
No, I get to fight with this berserk monster all over Gotham, trying to keep it from hurting anyone.
Because I'm a hero!
Right.
This isn't what I'm supposed to be doing. What I'm supposed to be doing is tracking some sort of weapon that the Black Mask is trying to get hold of, something Oracle caught wind of.
Not playing tag with something out of a horror movie. I don't do--
What the hell?
HEY! HEY!
Dammit! What is his problem?
It's like he's ignoring me.
Man-Bat's been tearing through the East Side all morning, but he's too good to fight me?
Where's he go--
Uh-oh.
I hate this city.

BEFORE.
♪
'SCUSE ME--
FATHER?
OH, HELLO.
CAN I HELP YOU, FRIEND?
YEAH... YOU CAN.
SHUK
HNNN...
FATHER MARK'S FIRST NIGHT IN GOTHAM.

ORACLE'S HEADQUARTERS, NOW.
DO! NOT! HURT! HIM!
I HEARD YOU THE FIRST SEVEN TIMES, ORACLE!
IF YOU DIDN'T WANT HIM HURT, YOU SHOULDN'T HAVE PUT ME ON HIM.
TRUST ME, HUNTRESS...I DIDN'T HAVE ANY OTHER CHOICE. YOU WERE MY CLOSEST OPERATIVE.
THIS NEEDS TO GET CONTAINED, AND NOW!
ROBIN'S ON THE OTHER END OF GOTHAM, TRYING TO TRACK DOWN LANGSTROM'S WIFE. BATMAN'S HEADED TO THE BARRACKS TO FIND LANGSTROM'S SERUM.
SOMETHING'S NOT RIGHT... IT'S LIKE HE'S AFTER SOMETHING...
WELL, RIGHT NOW HE'S LOOKING FOR A MEAL.
WHAT HAPPENED TO YOU, KIRK?
SURE, WORRY ABOUT HIM. THIS THING'S ALMOST KILLED ME FIVE DIFFERENT WAYS.
WHEN DID YOU BECOME SUCH A COMPLAINER, HELENA?
DON'T MAKE ME HURT YOU, TOO.

Know what makes a horrible situation worse? A stampede of **panicked idiots.**
People invariably pick the wrong way to run, every time.

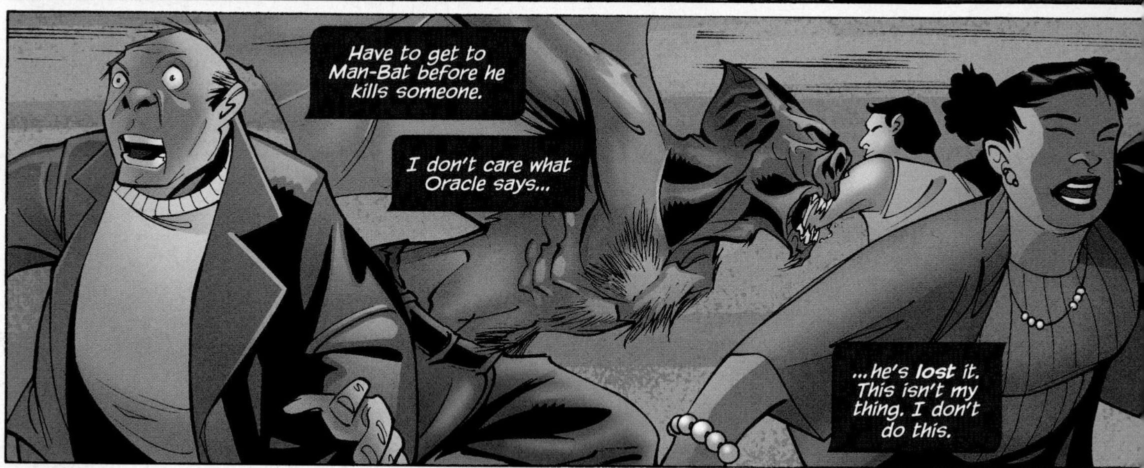
Have to get to Man-Bat before he kills someone.
I don't care what Oracle says...
...he's **lost** it. This isn't my thing. I don't do this.

If Dick doesn't get back with that serum...
Strange... he's got people all around him, but he's not **focusing** on any of them.

Oh, God. Strike that.

He's focused now. That girl is dead.
She can't even move.

SKREEE
Dammit.

Consider the non-lethal options exhausted.
SHUNK

KAIIIIIEE!
CHOK

That's what he gets for turning his back on--

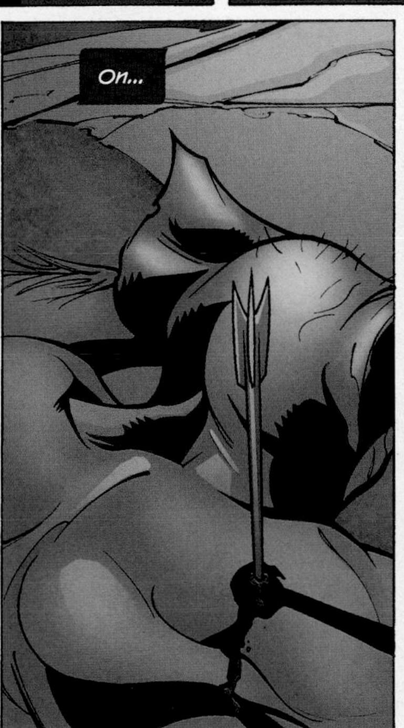
On...

HSSSSS

Uh-oh.
Well, at least he knows I'm here now.

IN THE WEEKS FOLLOWING FATHER MARK'S STABBING, GOTHAM CITY FELL VICTIM TO THE **CLENCH VIRUS**. THE EAST END WAS HIT THE HARDEST.
BUT FATHER MARK'S FAITH HELD.

AND WHEN A **CATACLYSMIC EARTHQUAKE** SHOOK GOTHAM, FATHER MARK'S FAITH REMAINED STRONG.

FOLLOWING THE QUAKE, A GANG WAR RIPPED THROUGH THE **NO MAN'S LAND** THAT GOTHAM BECAME.
AND STILL, FATHER MARK BELIEVED.

THE FIRST VISIBLE CRACKS IN FATHER MARK'S FAITH STARTED TO APPEAR WHEN EVIL GODS FROM ANOTHER DIMENSION INVADED THE PLANET.

WHEN GOTHAM'S GREATEST PROTECTOR WAS FEARED DEAD, GANGS AND THE INSANE SWEPT OVER GOTHAM.
FATHER MARK WATCHED ONCE AGAIN, AS GOTHAM PUSHED HIM TO THE BRINK.

HE WATCHED AS THE LEVIATHAN TRIED TO BURN HIS FAITH DOWN AROUND HIM.

UHNN!
SKEEEE
I should have killed him when I had the chance.
That thought, I can't get rid of it.
And every time I leave one of them alive...be it a mobster or one of Arkham's monsters...
...that's one more animal that's going to be back on the streets, just waiting to destroy a life.
Never been this close to Langstrom before...it's overwhelming. The breath, the heat, the screeching...
I know Oracle and Batman don't approve of me. And right now, I don't care.

This is going to **hurt.**
I have to believe that if Kirk Langstrom was any kind of man...

Got it!
THAP
If he was any kind of man, he'd want to be put out of his misery.

He'd see the monster he'd become, and he'd **want** someone to put him down. Before he killed someone.
Like me, for instance. God, he's fast. This is going to be close.

The others don't see it.

They wait for a cure. They hope for rehabilitation. They pretend the system works.
But they all know it doesn't. They know there is **no cure.**

They have faith in these monsters, but not in me.
UHN!
Dammit... Man-Bat's what... four hundred pounds? If I go hand-to-hand with this thing, it's going to tear me--
Ahhh, screw it.
RAAAA!
WHAM
HURNN!
COME ON, LANGSTROM! DO YOU HEAR ME, MONSTER?
COME ON!
Wait... something's happening. He's... he's...
What... the... hell?!

NO. THIS IS NOT HAPPENING.
There is no way I am letting this thing go.
There is no way this monster hurts someone because I failed.
THUMP

So I'll do what Batman wouldn't.
What Oracle can't.
Langstrom crossed the line.
He has to be dealt with.
Permanently. No matter what.
That's what I believe in.

...YOUR FATHER. MAY THE MYSTERY I CELEBRATE HELP ME TO...TO...
PLEASE...HELP ME. HELP ME UNDERSTAND.
IF I'M BEING TESTED... THERE'S BEEN SO MUCH...IT'S BEEN SO *HORRIBLE*... THIS PLACE...
I NEED TO KNOW. PLEASE, GOD, IF THIS IS YOUR PLAN, I NEED *SOMETHING*.
I'VE GOT NOTHING LEFT. SO IF YOU'RE TESTING ME, WHAT ELSE DO I NEED TO DO?!
I NEED YOUR GUIDANCE!
CRASH

LORD...
I AM HERE, MY CHILD.
NO... THAT'S NOT...
BELIEVE IN ME, AS I BELIEVE IN YOU. YOUR FAITH HAS BEEN REWARDED. LOOK UPON THEM, MY CHILD.
THIS BEAST...
...THIS HARLOT.
KILL THEM. PROVE YOUR DEVOTION TO ME.
YOUR GOD COMMANDS YOU. KILL THEM BOTH.
THANK YOU.

TEN HOURS AGO.
THE GOTHAM PIERS.
DO YOU HAVE IT?
YUH-YES... I HAVE IT. I JUST...I JUST... CAN YOU SHOW ME...DID YOU BRING THE MONEY?
OPEN THE CASE, DOCTOR KETOLA.
WE'D HEARD THAT THE GOVERNMENT WAS, THAT THEY WERE GOING TO--
THE PROJECT IS GOING TO GET TAKEN OVER BY THE GOVERNMENT. THAT WE'D BE SHUT DOWN.
THAT WE'D GET NOTHING.
THIS IS THE ONLY PROTOTYPE. IT WORKS, BUT THERE COULD BE SIDE EFFECTS...WE HAVEN'T TESTED FOR PROLONGED EXPOSURE...
THAT'S QUITE ALL RIGHT, DOCTOR. JUST OPEN THE CASE.
WHAT ARE YOU GOING TO DO WITH IT?
THP THP
HURK--*
I'M GOING TO KILL PEOPLE WITH IT.

NOW.
I'M NOT QUESTIONING YOU, I'M JUST POINTING OUT THAT YOU'VE MADE A *MASSIVE* TACTICAL ERROR. IT'S A POOR USE OF RESOURCES.
I HAVE EXPERIENCE WITH MAN-BAT. I SHOULD BE THERE, NOT ACROSS TOWN CHECKING ON HIS WIDOW.
MAN-BAT'S NOT DEAD, ROBIN.
TT! SEE? YOU SHOULD HAVE SENT ME.
THIS IS WHAT I PUT UP WITH, ORACLE.
HE'S A CHARMER, ALL RIGHT.
ANY SIGN OF THEM?
NOTHING.
HUNTRESS AND MAN-BAT TEAR ACROSS THE CITY, THEN BOTH DISAPPEAR.
I EXPECTED PROLONGED SCREAMING, EXPLOSIONS, AND BLOODY MURDER.
I TOLD YOU, MAN-BAT CAN CONTROL IT NOW.
I WAS TALKING ABOUT HUNTRESS.

I don't think about the pain. Although there's plenty of that.

The details are fuzzy. I remember falling. Glass. But that doesn't matter. Just killing Man-Bat.

I don't think about the sound of praying.

Although there's something off about it. And I can't move my arms.

The voice sounds a little...manic. Then I notice that the man praying, it's a priest...he's got a crazy look in his eye. And a shotgun.

Both are kind of troublesome. But I can ignore all that.

All I can think about is that I am going to freaking **kill** Man-Bat.

Of course, I don't see Man-Bat.

Oh, wait.
BATMAN STREETS OF GOTHAM
LEVIATHAN
PART 2 OF 2

I think I might be in trouble here.
Need a few minutes... think this through. Maybe he didn't see that I woke up.
I SEE YOU, SERPENT!
Or maybe he did.

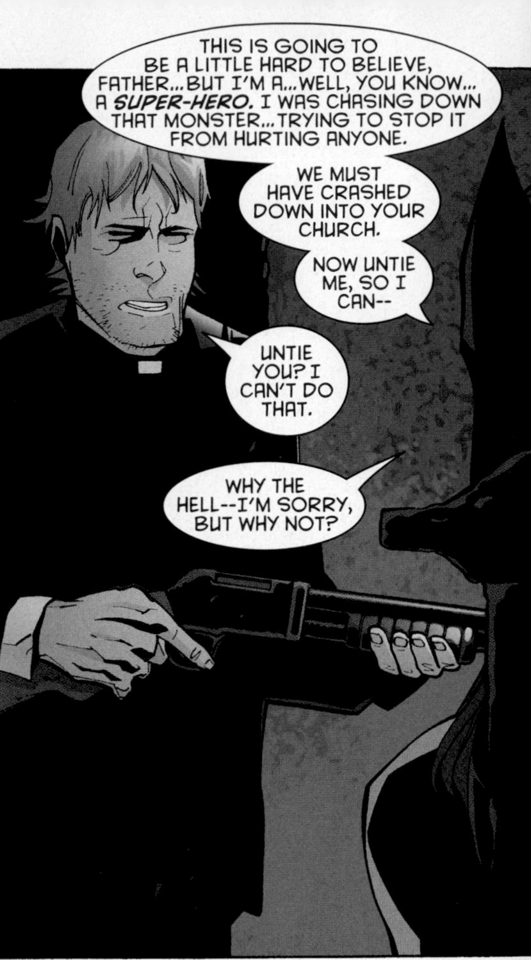
THIS IS GOING TO BE A LITTLE HARD TO BELIEVE, FATHER... BUT I'M A... WELL, YOU KNOW... A SUPER-HERO. I WAS CHASING DOWN THAT MONSTER... TRYING TO STOP IT FROM HURTING ANYONE.
WE MUST HAVE CRASHED DOWN INTO YOUR CHURCH.
NOW UNTIE ME, SO I CAN--
UNTIE YOU? I CAN'T DO THAT.
WHY THE HELL--I'M SORRY, BUT WHY NOT?

BECAUSE I'M GOING TO KILL YOU. YOU AND THE BEAST.
THE LEVIATHAN.

I. Am having. The WORST. Day.
...WHY WOULD YOU DO THAT?

BECAUSE GOD TOLD ME TO.
HE TOLD ME TO KILL THE HARLOT AND THE BEAST.
And in all honesty, I don't know what upsets me more. The killing bit, or that he called me a tramp.

GOD IS TESTING ME.
EVER SINCE I CAME TO GOTHAM, I'VE BEEN TESTED. BY CRIME, BY VIOLENCE, BY NATURAL DISASTERS, BY EVIL...
...AND NOW GOD HAS ANOTHER TEST FOR ME.
He's crazy. I don't know what's happened to this man, but he's lost it.
HOW WOULD GOD FEEL IF YOU JUST KILLED MAN-BAT? LOOK, WE CAN TALK ABOUT THIS...

LORD! YOUR SERVANT NEEDS ANOTHER SIGN!

DO NOT LISTEN TO THE TEMPTRESS'S LIES, MY CHILD.
KILL HER. KILL THE BEAST.

...
Okay, maybe he's not crazy.
Please tell me that the voice of God didn't just boom through here and tell a priest to kill me.
Could this get any worse?

SKREEE
Yes, it could.

HURR... HURR...
LANGSTROM... LANGSTROM! PULL IT TOGETHER!
This is useless... he's nothing but an animal. Dammit!
Shotgun or not, Man-Bat is going to slaughter this guy.
LORD, PLEASE, JUST GIVE ME MORE TIME...
NO.

NINE HOURS AGO.
YOU KNOW THE NAMES.
YES.
YOU KNOW WHERE TO FIND THEM.
YES.

THEY ARE SINNERS. THEY MUST BE PUNISHED.
YES.

YOU CAN KILL WITH IMPUNITY. YOU ARE THE *ONLY ONE.*
DO YOU KNOW WHAT IT IS, TO KILL WITH IMPUNITY?

IT IS TO BE GOD.

GO FORTH. AND ONCE YOU HAVE KILLED THE SINNERS WE SPOKE OF...

...THEN PUNISH ANYONE YOU SEE FIT.

SKREEE
Langstrom's lost it.

SKREEE
SKREEE
He's about three seconds away from breaking through those ropes and slaughtering the priest.

Why? Why attack the priest? He's **ignored me** all day...and I put a crossbow bolt through him.
Why would he care about--

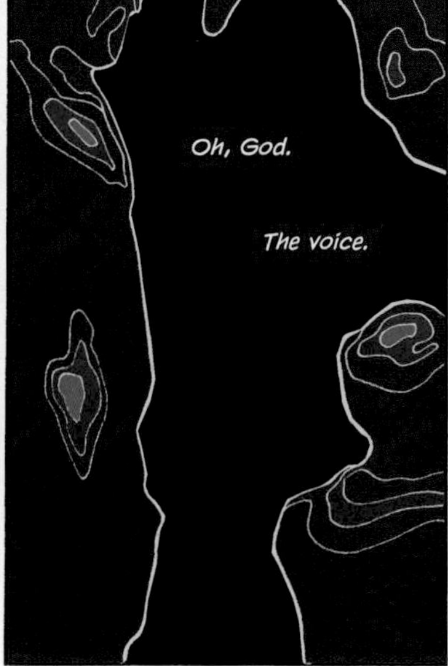
Oh, God.
The voice.

There's someone here.
There's someone else here, and Man-Bat can **see** him.

THE EAST END BUS DEPOT, GOTHAM CITY.

SIX HOURS AGO.

I JUST NEEDED TO GET AWAY.

I HEARD ABOUT A SPECIES OF BAT FROM THE SOUTH...LOUISIANA... AND THINGS GOT COMPLICATED.

FRANCINE, PLEASE...PLEASE JUST *TALK* TO ME. ARE THE KIDS--?

I'M SORRY...I'M SO SORRY...I'M TIRED.

WITH EVERYTHING I'VE GONE THROUGH, NOW THAT I CAN CONTROL THE CHANGE...I'VE BEEN STAYING MAN-BAT LONGER AND LONGER.

SOMETIMES, WHEN I STAY IN THAT FORM TOO LONG, I START TO...

AAAIEEEE!

I CAN FEEL THE ANIMAL TAKING OVER. FRANCINE, SOMETHING'S HAPPENING--

I DON'T...
SHLIKK

ARRGHH!

AAAHHH--*

NO... THAT'S NOT POSSIBLE...

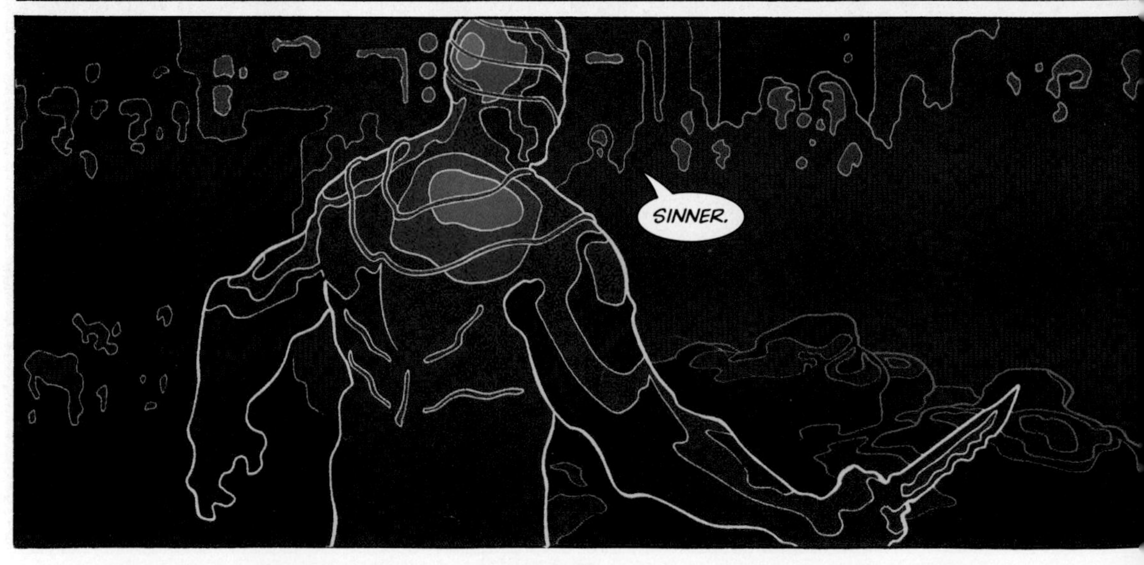
SINNER.

LORD! PROTECT ME!
GIVE ME YOUR STRENGTH!
I was going to do it. I was going to kill Man-Bat.

He was hunting something... and I was going to kill him.
LET ME HEAR YOUR VOICE! GIVE YOUR SERVANT HOPE!
LISTEN TO ME!
THAT'S NOT THE VOICE OF GOD, FATHER! YOU HAVE TO RUN! GET OUT OF HERE!

BE SILENT!
I AM TRYING TO COMMUNE WITH THE LORD!
God help me, had I actually managed to do it...

PLEASE, FATHER... I'M TRYING TO SAVE YOUR LIFE. YOU HAVE TO LISTEN!
Come on... come on...
PLEASE, FATHER! YOU'RE ABOUT TO MAKE A HORRIBLE MISTAKE... I ALMOST MADE THE SAME ONE... PLEASE, YOU HAVE TO RUN!

HEED THE WORD OF THE LORD, MY CHILD.
THE WOMAN SPEAKS LIES. I AM THE TRUTH. AND I DEMAND THE BEAST'S BLOOD.
YES, MY LORD...

SNAP
SNAP
Out of time.

SKREEE
THANK YOU, GOD.

There's no way I'm going to be able to hold him for long. He's too strong,
UHN!
FATHER, RUN!

Just have to get the priest out of the crossfire... find a way to pinpoint this voice, whoever he is...
I WILL NOT ABANDON... I WILL NOT...
LORD!
No... please...

LANGSTROM... PLEASE...
LANGSTROM, YOU HAVE TO HELP ME. I CAN'T DO THIS ALONE... PLEASE, KIRK, PROVE ME WRONG. TELL ME YOU'RE IN THERE.

LORD... WHY HAVE YOU ABANDONED ME?

Someone's going to die, right now.
PLEASE, GOD...

BEHIND... PRIEST...
KA-CHAK

GOD IS EVERYWHERE.
BLAM
BLAM BLAM
NYEARGHH!
SKREEE

UHN!
The voice has guns. Great.
If not for the sound, Man-Bat and I would be dead now. Crazy acoustics in this place.

CRASH
Like that.

Batman.
The second I see him, I know this is going to go exactly the wrong way.
He doesn't know.
He thinks we're still after Man-Bat.
SKREEE
THUD
The one person who can see the shooter.
SAY GOODNIGHT, LANGSTROM.
CHOK
HK!

BATMAN! FORGET MAN-BAT! WE'VE GOT A SHOOTER!
THE PRIEST IS--
ANOTHER ONE! HE'S INVISIBLE!

SCANNING.
VTT
But then, that's the great thing about Batman...

...he's ready for anything. Common thugs, super-people, aliens, gods...
Invisible means nothing.
HUNTRESS...

BANGBANG
BANGBANGBANGBANG
MOVE!

UHNN... NO...CAN'T SEE...

DID YOU SEE HIM?
NOT BEFORE HE STARTED SHOOTING. STILL CAN'T PINPOINT HIM... THE ACOUSTICS IN HERE AREN'T HELPING.
I WAS GLAD TO SEE LANGSTROM STILL ALIVE.

I... I ALMOST--
KA-CHAK
I FORGOT TO TELL YOU ABOUT THE PRIEST.

WHAT OF THIS ONE, LORD?

DO YOU WANT *HIM* DEAD, TOO?
VTT
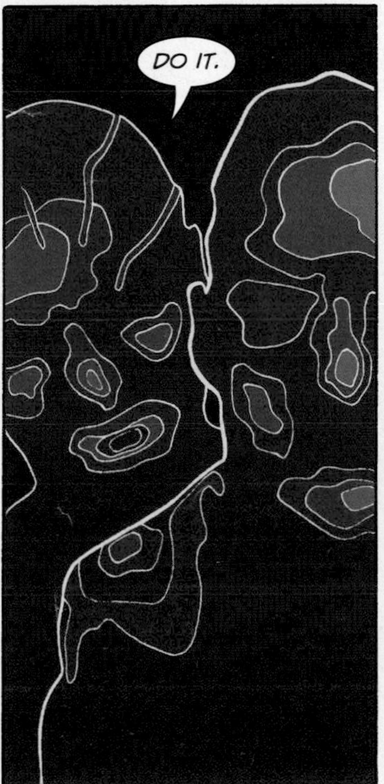
*DO IT.*

*KILL THEM ALL.*

KRRAKK
AACK!

HNN!
KRAZZ
FZZT

THUD

WHAT JUST HAPPENED?
I HAVE NO IDEA.

FATHER?
I TAKE IT ONE OF YOU HAS THE ABILITY TO CALL THE POLICE?
THIS IDIOT SHOWED UP ABOUT TWO MINUTES BEFORE YOU AND THE GIANT RAT.
I'M SORRY...I SAW HIM, BUT I WAS TOO TIRED. I'D BEEN STAYING AS MAN-BAT TOO LONG. I LOST CONTROL.
I TRIED SO HARD...
LANGSTROM. KIRK. IT'S OKAY. YOU DID GOOD.
I'M SORRY IF I...IF I HURT YOU.
YOU WERE TRYING TO SAVE LIVES. ORACLE TOLD ME YOU HAD CHANGED. THAT YOU HAD MORE CONTROL.
I DIDN'T LISTEN.
FATHER...I THOUGHT...
YOU THINK I HAVEN'T SEEN THIS KIND OF THING BEFORE? I COULDN'T GET A BEAD ON HIM BECAUSE OF THE SOUND IN HERE.
I TRIED TO KEEP HIM TALKING.
YOU RISKED YOUR LIFE WITH THAT LITTLE GAMBIT. QUITE THE LEAP OF FAITH.
THIS IS GOTHAM, SWEETHEART. *HAVING* FAITH ISN'T ENOUGH.
IN GOTHAM, YOU HAVE TO FIGHT TO *KEEP* IT.
END

IN THE BLEAK MIDWINTER
CHRISTMAS EVE.
Just like everywhere else in the country, Gotham drivers get more aggressive around the holidays.
BOOOM
One big difference, Gotham has **us** to pull drivers to safety before their burning cars **explode**.

WE'VE NOTIFIED PARAMEDICS, BUT IT LOOKS LIKE YOU AND YOUR PARTNER ARE GOING TO BE OKAY.
THANKS. WE WERE RAMMED OFF THE ROAD BY ANOTHER VEHICLE. WHILE WE LAY THERE BLEEDING, THE PERP *TOOK OFF*.
DID YOU SEE WHO ATTACKED YOU?
OH, YEAH... *HEH*.
SOME-THING FUNNY, OFFICER RANDALL?
GOTHAM-FUNNY.
NOT ONLY WERE WE SIDESWIPED BY A THREE-WAY MIX OF A CAR, A SNOWPLOW AND A SLEIGH, BUT THE PERP TOOK OFF WITH ALL OUR TOYS.
TOYS?
USED TOYS DONATED FOR UNDERPRIVILEGED KIDS. POLICE VOLUNTEERS WERE GOING TO REPAIR THEM.
DARE I ASK ***WHO*** TOOK THEM?
HO HO HO.

I FIGURED IT WAS JUST A MATTER OF TIME BEFORE *SANTA* JOINED OUR ROGUES GALLERY.
RIGHT, BECAUSE YOU'RE OBVIOUSLY WAY TOO GROWN UP FOR CHRISTMAS.
NAH, I LIKE IT FINE. MOTHER USUALLY ETS ME SOMETHING-- ETLINER, HYDROFOIL, I GOT A PRIVATE ISLAND LAST YEAR--
AND I USED TO THINK IT WAS A BIG CHRISTMAS IF BRUCE ALLOWED ALFRED TO MAKE EGGNOG.
YOU GET BETTER STUFF IF YOU'RE A *REAL SON.*
AH.

GENTLY DOES IT, LET'S TRY IT AGAIN...
HRRRRRMM
ALMOST GOT IT...
KRAK
BASH
SKREE
THINK THAT'S IT...
KLICK
POOM
BOTHER.
TRY, TRY AGAIN. I DIDN'T MEAN TO MAKE SUCH A FUSS.

BROKE MY CAR. BROKE THE POLICEMAN'S CAR.
BROKE THE POLICEMEN, TOO. SAD ABOUT THAT.
DIDN'T MEAN TO. I NEVER DO.
BUT THEY CAN EASILY BE PUT BACK TOGETHER AGAIN. THEY *ALL* CAN.
BESIDES, I NEED THE TOYS FOR THE CHILDREN. THE *TOYS* WILL MAKE IT ALL RIGHT.

WHRRRM
NEED A HAND, ST. NICK?
OH. THANKS, NO NEED. I'M ALMOST DONE. I'M LATE FOR A PARTY WITH LITTLE ONES.
IT'S OKAY, SANTA. I'VE BEEN A GOOD BOY THIS YEAR. MAYBE YOU CAN DO ME A FAVOR IN RETURN...
I'M TRYING TO GET TO SOME KIDS, MYSELF. SEEMS A BUNCH OF THEM HAVE DISAPPEARED LATELY FROM GOTHAM ORPHANAGES AND SHELTERS.
THAT'S TOO BAD...
ISN'T IT? YOU WOULDN'T KNOW ANYTHING ABOUT THAT, WOULD YOU?
ER...

WHAM
YEAH, I'M THINKING YOU *MIGHT*.

I'M SO LATE.

AAGH!

THAT'S THE HOLIDAY SPIRIT FOR YOU.

SANTA, YOU JUST MADE MY NAUGHTY LIST.

QUIETLY, NOW. NOT A CREATURE STIRRING, AND ALL...

AH. LOOK AT THE LITTLE ANGELS.

I'M SORRY THE TOYS ARE NOT QUITE RIGHT...

...BUT I PUT THEM TOGETHER AS BEST I COULD...

WITH A BIT OF IMAGINATION THEY'LL BE GOOD AS NEW.

AND MAYBE IF *THEY'RE* GOOD AS NEW, THEN *YOU'LL* BE--
HELLO, HUMPTY.

HELLO, BATMAN. MERRY CHRISTMAS.

MERRY CHRISTMAS. A WHILE BACK WE MET WITH YOUR FRIEND, *THE BROKER*.
OH DEAR. I HOPE YOU WEREN'T TOO HARD ON HIM.

HE'LL RECOVER. WE LEARNED YOU WERE CONSIDERING LEAVING ARKHAM FOR A PLACE OF YOUR OWN.

BROKER HAD EARMARKED YOU FOR THIS SHELTER, SO WE DECIDED TO TRY HERE FIRST.
WHY A CHILDREN'S SHELTER, HUMPTY? WHAT ARE YOU UP TO?

ALL I WANTED TO DO WAS TO MAKE A NICE HOME FOR THE CHILDREN I FOUND--
"YOU FOUND"?
LET HIM TALK, ROBIN.

...FOR THE CHILDREN I FOUND, AND GIVE THEM A BIT OF CHRISTMAS.

THAT'S ALL WELL AND GOOD, HUMPTY, BUT YOU CAN'T JUST COME INTO AN ORPHANAGE WITHOUT PERMISSION. AND YOU CERTAINLY CAN'T--
I'M TALKING, ROBIN.
WAIT A MINUTE...

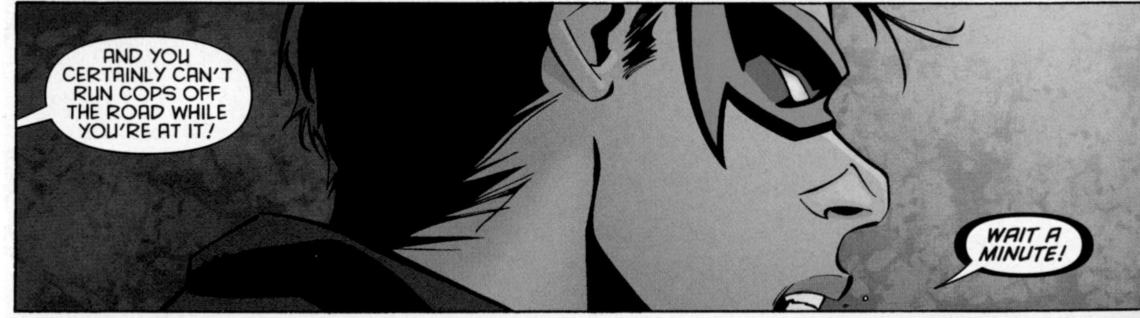
AND YOU CERTAINLY CAN'T RUN COPS OFF THE ROAD WHILE YOU'RE AT IT!
WAIT A MINUTE!

WHAT?
THE LIGHTS ARE ON. WE'RE TALKING. I JUST YELLED.

I NOTICED.
NONE OF THESE KIDS HAVE SAID SO MUCH AS "BOO."

OH, GOD.

SHE'S DEAD. THEY'RE ALL DEAD.
OH, HUMPTY...

DID YOU DO THIS?!
NO, I--

HUMPTY, YOU'D BETTER EXPLAIN THIS FAST.
I FOUND THE CHILDREN ALREADY LIKE THAT! I GATHER UP BROKEN THINGS FROM TRASH DUMPS TO PUT THEM BACK TOGETHER AGAIN.

YOU FOUND THEM IN A DUMP?
NO...

"...I WAS SEARCHING FOR PARTS NEAR THE RIVER WHEN ONE OF THE BROKEN CHILDREN FLOATED UP TO ME.
"I TOOK HIM WITH ME, BUT THE NEXT DAY, ANOTHER ONE CAME UP, TOO...
"...AND SHE WASN'T ALONE."
I WAS SO SAD THAT THE CHILDREN WERE KILLED SO CLOSE TO CHRISTMAS. I THOUGHT MAYBE IF I GAVE THEM CHRISTMAS, AND FIXED THE TOYS FOR THEM, THEN MAYBE... MAYBE...

HUMPTY, NOTHING'S GOING TO BE ABLE TO "PUT THE CHILDREN TOGETHER AGAIN."
...
...I KNOW.

BUT MAYBE SOMEONE ELSE CAN FIX IT...
WE'LL DO WHAT WE CAN.
GCPD. COME IN. WE NEED A POLICE VAN, AND A... A...

YOU GOING TO BE OKAY?

HELLO?
THIS IS BATMAN. NEED A POLICE VAN TO THE RAINBOW HOUSE SHELTER, AND A FEW VEHICLES FROM THE CORONER'S OFFICE.

I'LL GET THE MONSTER THAT DID THIS.
WE'LL GET HIM.

The sight of those kids... **horrible.**
Can't blame Robin for losing it.

I **knew** some of those kids. Runaways. They'd say things couldn't be any worse out there than at home.

Any worse, indeed.
But how many times was I tempted to do the same thing? It could've been **me.**

Stop. Can't think like that. Need to focus.

I'm definitely not gonna get any help from Batman, which means I'm going to be tracking this killer down **myself.**

WHO'S THERE?
SLAM

COLIN, DID YOU SEE A STRANGE MAN?
NO, SISTER. I'VE BEEN IN MY ROOM ALL NIGHT.

HOW ODD... I MUST HAVE IMAGINED IT.

SISTER AGNES?

SISTER AGNES, WHERE WERE YOU? IT'S ALMOST MIDNIGHT MASS.
COMING!

"Past Three o'clock, On a cold frosty morning...

"...Past three o'clock, Good morrow masters all."

"Born is a baby Gentle as may be, Son of the Eternal Father supernal."

"Seraph choir singeth,
Angel bell ringeth,
Hark how they rhyme it,
Time it and chime it!"
"Mid earth rejoices
Hearing such voices.
Ne'ertofore so well
Caroling nowell!"
"Light out of star-land
Leadeth from far land..."
"Princes, to meet him,
Worship and greet him."

"Myrrh from full coffer,
Incense they offer;
Nor is the golden
Nugget withholden."

"Past three o'clock,
On a cold frosty morning..."

THE WINNER OF THE PREVIOUS MATCH FIGHTS THE NEWCOMER.
WHOEVER WINS THAT MATCH MOVES ON TO THE FINAL ROUND.
WHOEVER WINS THE FINAL MATCH GAINS THEIR *FREEDOM*...
EXCEPT THE FINAL MATCH IS AGAINST *ME*.

GOTHAM CITY.
THE SPRANG RIVER WALK.

MMMMM...

'NIGHT, GORGEOUS.

EH?
ACCKK!
SLASH
WHAT DO YA WANT? TAKE MY WALLET--
NO... NO!

THIS MEAT SCULPTURE USED TO BE *FRANK HOHIMER*...
...PROFESSIONAL SAFECRACKER.
FRANK HAD THE MIDAS TOUCH. SPECIALIZED IN HIGH-PROFILE DIAMOND JOBS.
NOT EXACTLY A MAJOR LOSS TO MANKIND.
BESIDES THE POINT.
GOTHAM

WE'RE KEEPING IT QUIET DOWNTOWN, BUT THIS IS THE *FIFTH* SUCH KILLING IN THE PAST THREE WEEKS.
EACH VICTIM HAD AN EXTENSIVE CRIMINAL HISTORY-- NO CONNETION TO ONE ANOTHER.

FINGER-PRINTS?
NONE.
INJURIES?
VICTIM'S THROAT WAS SLASHED. STOMACH GOUGED. SPINE SNAPPED. REAL MESS.
SCREAMS PERSONAL. KILLER KNEW THE VICTIM.
INDEED.
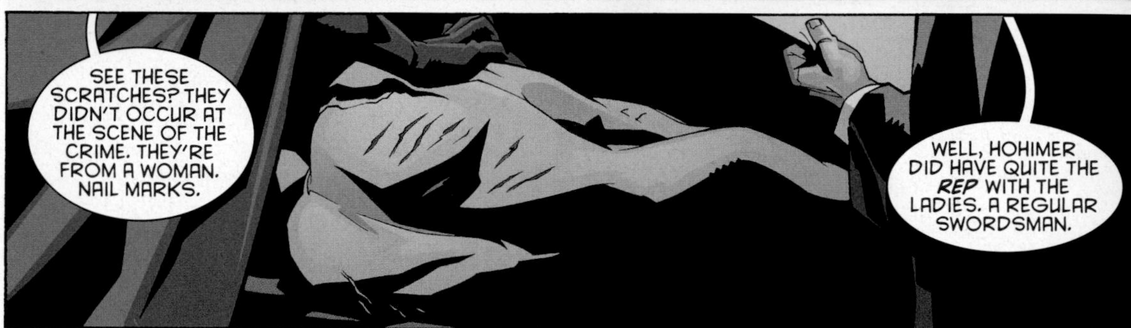
SEE THESE SCRATCHES? THEY DIDN'T OCCUR AT THE SCENE OF THE CRIME. THEY'RE FROM A WOMAN. NAIL MARKS.
WELL, HOHIMER DID HAVE QUITE THE *REP* WITH THE LADIES. A REGULAR SWORDSMAN.

FINGERS WERE SEVERED IN A DEFENSIVE POSTURE. ANGLE SUGGESTS VICTIM WAS HOLDING HIS HAND UPWARDS. OUR MAN HAD *SIZE* TO HIM.
ANYTHING TAKEN OFF THE BODY?

HERE.

MONEY. CREDIT CARDS STILL INTACT. COUPLE OF BUSINESS CARDS.

THIS MEAN ANYTHING TO YOU?
ASIDE FROM TACKY, NO.

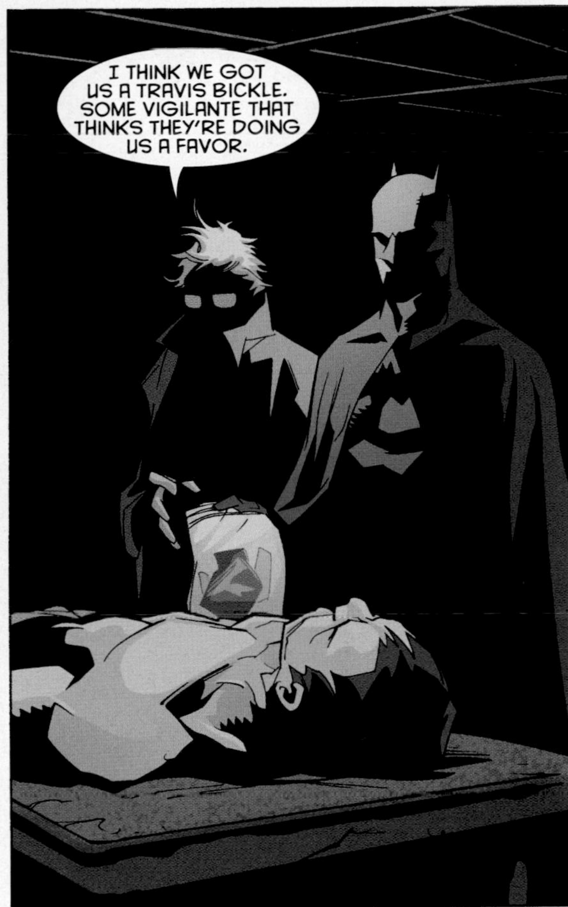
I THINK WE GOT US A TRAVIS BICKLE. SOME VIGILANTE THAT THINKS THEY'RE DOING US A FAVOR.

MAYBE HE IS.

MAYBE I'M LOSING MY HEARING BECAUSE I DIDN'T CATCH THAT.
RUN ALL VIOLENT CRIMES FOR THE PAST COUPLE OF MONTHS. CHECK OUT DESPONDENT FAMILY MEMBERS.
ANYONE WITH A GRUDGE TO SETTLE THAT'S BEEN VOCAL.
AND FOR KICKS, HAVE YOUR BOYS CHECK ON ANY RECENT MISSING ASYLUM PATIENTS.
WILL DO.

MICKEY'S IRISH TAVERN.
CHARLIE.
WHAT THE HELL--?!
GOT A SECOND?
WHAT DO YOU WANT?
JUST A FEW QUESTIONS ANSWERED.
FORGET IT. HAVEN'T RUN WITH THE MONGOLS IN OVER TWO YEARS.
GOOD TO HEAR. NOT WHY I'M HERE, THOUGH.

I'M AWARE OF YOUR RECENT LOSS. I UNDERSTAND YOUR ANGER.
OH, *YOU* DO?
WADING THROUGH THE ATROCITIES I'VE SEEN, WATCHING INNOCENT PEOPLE DIE, YOU LEARN TO HARNESS THE RAGE AND CUT EVERYTHING ELSE LOOSE.

SHOVE OFF.

YOU LOST YOUR WIFE TO SOME LOWLIFE DIRTBAG WHO GOT OFF ON A TECHNICALITY. AND WHILE YOUR WIFE LIES SIX FEET UNDER, *HE* GETS TO BREATHE THE SAME AIR YOU DO.
YOU'RE DOING A *BAD JOB* OF CALMING ME DOWN.
SOMEONE'S KILLING UNDESIRABLES. THIEVES. STICKUP MEN.
CRY ME A RIVER.

YOU KNOW ANYTHING ABOUT IT, CHARLIE?
YOU ACCUSING *ME?*
JUST MAKING THE ROUNDS. TALKING TO PEOPLE WITH POTENTIAL MOTIVES.
YOU MADE IT VERY CLEAR TO A LOT OF PEOPLE, YOU WERE GOING TO TAKE *ACTION*.
QUITE FRANKLY, I DON'T BLAME YOU. BUT IT WOULDN'T MAKE IT RIGHT.

YOU WANNA KNOW THE *TRUTH?* I GOT A TWELVE-YEAR-OLD GIRL WHO'S GONE THROUGH TOO MUCH GRIEF AS IT IS.
I DO ANOTHER STRETCH IN BLACKGATE AND SHE'LL TURN TO DANCING IN CLUBS...AND I *CAN'T* HAVE THAT.
AND AS MUCH AS I'D GET OFF PUTTING A CAP IN SOME LOWLIFE'S HEAD, IT AIN'T GONNA BRING KAREN BACK.
SO TAKE ME AT MY WORD OR DO WHAT YOU GOTTA DO.

GO.

THAT'S IT?

YOU'RE TELLING THE TRUTH. I'VE BEEN MONITORING YOUR HEART RATE.

WHOEVER'S KILLING THESE PUNKS, I'M GONNA SAY A *PRAYER* FOR THEM TONIGHT. I'M GONNA PRAY THEY CONTINUE TO KILL AS *MANY* OF THESE ORGAN DONORS AS THEY CAN GET TO.
AND WHEN I'M DONE, I'M GONNA PRAY YOU DON'T STOP 'EM.

Sometimes the lines get blurred. Sometimes the only difference between you and them is the mask and cape.

THE WAREHOUSE DISTRICT.
GET THESE MEN OUT OF HERE BEFORE THEY CONTAMINATE THE SCENE.
YOU MEAN THE DETECTIVES?
WHY'S HE HERE?
DON'T WORRY ABOUT IT, McINTYRE. JUST DO YOUR JOB.
YOU SURE KNOW HOW TO MAKE FRIENDS AND INSPIRE PEOPLE.
WHO FOUND THE BODY?
COUPLA KIDS. SMELLED SOMETHING "RANK."
NO SIGN OF A STRUGGLE. NO BLOOD TRAILS. BODY WAS CLEARLY DUMPED HERE. LIGATURE MARKS ON THE WRISTS SUGGEST HANDCUFFS.

WHAT'S THAT?
PUPA STAGE TWO.

YOU MIND TRANSLATING?
IT'S THE STAGE OF LARVA METAMORPHOSIS. IF I HAD TO BET--VICTIM'S BEEN POSTMORTEM FOUR DAYS.

THAT CHECKS OUT. WIFE FILED A MISSING PERSONS THREE DAYS AGO.

VICTIM'S NAME: MARCUS FEINBERG. PLASTIC SURGEON. SPECIALIZED IN BREAST AUGMENTATION. SAD DAY FOR POLE DANCERS.
FORTY-THREE YEARS OLD. NO CRIMINAL HISTORY. LIVED IN THE 'BURBS WITH HIS YOUNG WIFE. TAUGHT AT GOTHAM MEMORIAL.
DON'T SEE ANY CONNECTIONS TO OTHERS.

THINK IT'S TIME I MADE A HOUSE CALL OF MY OWN.

Getting into the doctor's office was no problem.
DOOMP
CLICK
The password took less than a minute to crack.
The harder chore was sifting through medical files, golf tips and travel itineraries.
Trying to shed any light on a connection.
Some link between the good doctor and the others.

And then it came gift wrapped in a little black dress.
BINGO.
I didn't recognize it before, but the image was now clear. The girl on the card was **Qetesh**--the Egyptian Goddess of goodness and beauty.
Also known as a Sex Goddess. The Pamela Anderson of her day.
I'LL HAVE THE NUMBERS TRACED AND SEE IF ANYTHING OF INTEREST COMES UP.
With an address I had a solid starting point.
Held properly you could hear a pin drop a block away.
Only I wasn't listening for a pin. I was listening for a name.

GRANFALLOON.
It was time to switch gears.
Change my persona.
GRANFALLOON.

Gotham was known for its nightlife. The city had many different sides to it.
Some quite ordinary. Others, one could say were quite... extreme. Exotic.

This place was an anomaly. A lavish club where the rich and powerful got to mingle with the sick and deviant under one roof.
There were familiar faces. Captains of industry. High powered lawyers. Mobsters. Sex offenders.
All rubbing shoulders. All looking to get their rocks off in whatever way suited them.
HEY, LOVE. HAVING A GOOD TIME?
NOT YET. BUT HOPEFULLY THAT'LL CHANGE NOW THAT YOU'RE HERE. GOT A NAME?
BENEDITA.
BENEDITA. THAT'S AN UNUSUAL NAME.
IT'S PORTUGUESE. IT MEANS BLESSED. IT'S ALSO MY WORKING NAME.
AND YOURS?
JAMES.
WOULD YOU LIKE TO SIT AND TALK, JAMES?
LOVE TO.

SO, HOW CAN I MAKE YOUR DREAMS COME TRUE?
I'M LOOKING FOR SOMETHING A LITTLE OFF THE MENU.
OH? DO TELL.

MY TASTE IS ON THE DARK SIDE.
CLEARLY.
SOMETIMES PLEASURE COMES FROM OTHER PLACES. YOU EVER HEAR THE BEST PART OF THE JOURNEY IS NOT THE END, BUT THE STRUGGLE? THE PAIN.

KINKY.
UNFORTUNATELY, DOLL, THAT'S NOT MY THING.

SHAME. I KNOW WE'D GET ALONG REAL WELL. OH, WELL. DIFFERENT STROKES. MAYBE YOU CAN MAKE AN INTRODUCTION? I'D BE ETERNALLY GRATEFUL.
IT'S A POSSIBILITY. YOU GOT A TYPE, JAMES? ANYTHING FLOATS YOUR BOAT?
IF I HAD MY DRUTHERS, SHE'D BE ON THE EXOTIC SIDE. DARK HAIR... SPANISH.

AH, SPICY. WELL, I JUST MIGHT BE ABLE TO ACCOMMODATE YOU.

It wasn't long before she showed up on a silver platter.
HAVE FUN.
SEE YOU AROUND, BENEDITA.
I REALLY HOPE SO.
SO, BENEDITA SAYS YOU LIKE TO PLAY ROUGH?
EVERY ONCE IN A WHILE I LIKE TO MIX THINGS UP.
SPICE OF LIFE, HUH?
SO WHAT NOW?
HAVE YOU BEEN HERE BEFORE?
NO.
WHO SPONSORED YOU?
A CERTAIN WEATHER MAN.
MAY I ASK WHAT YOU DO?
I'M IN THE IMPORT-EXPORT BUSINESS.
OH? WHAT DO YOU IMPORT-EXPORT?
YOU ASK A LOT OF QUESTIONS, BUT YOU'RE NOT ASKING ME WHAT YOU REALLY WANT TO KNOW.
SO WHY DON'T YOU CUT TO IT. I WON'T BITE UNLESS YOU ASK.
USUALLY I DO A LITTLE DUE DILIGENCE BEFORE I JUMP IN WITH A STRANGER.
MAKE SURE I KNOW WHO I'M MINGLING WITH. THAT THEY AREN'T A MANIC OR WORSE YET, VICE.

UNDERSTANDABLE. MY CARD. IF YOU GET ME A PEN I CAN WRITE DOWN SOME REFERENCES.
THIS'LL DO. BE BACK IN TWO SHAKES OF A RABBIT'S TAIL.
GLAD EVERYTHING CHECKED OUT.
OCCUPATIONAL HAZARD. DON'T BE OFFENDED. IT WAS FOR MY PROTECTIO AND YOURS.
NO OFFENSE TAKEN.
GOOD. LET'S GO, THEN.
NOT SO FAST.
NO! WHAT ARE YOU--?

URK!
WANNA TRY THAT WITH ME?
JAMES...

GGAAARRRR...

NO! DON'T HURT HIM! HE WAS PROTECTING ME! LET HIM GO!

SHE'LL ONLY BRING YOU MISERY AND PAIN!

COME ON, JAMES. LET'S GO.

I-I'M SO SORRY THAT HAPPENED. I CAN'T BELIEVE IT...
WHO WAS THAT?

A-AN EX-BOYFRIEND. HE USED TO BOUNCE AT THE CLUB. HE'S AN IDIOT.

CLEARLY. WHAT DOES HE WANT WITH YOU?
I DON'T KNOW. HE--JAMES, PLEASE. CAN'T WE JUST FORGET THAT HAPPENED?
I KNOW IT'S A DAMPER, BUT I PROMISE HE WON'T BOTHER US AGAIN. LET'S JUST HAVE A GOOD TIME, OKAY?

CONSIDER IT FORGOTTEN.

HEY, ANTHONY.
MA'AM. EVENING.

The waters had
been chummed.

It was now a
matter of waiting.

Waiting for the strike.

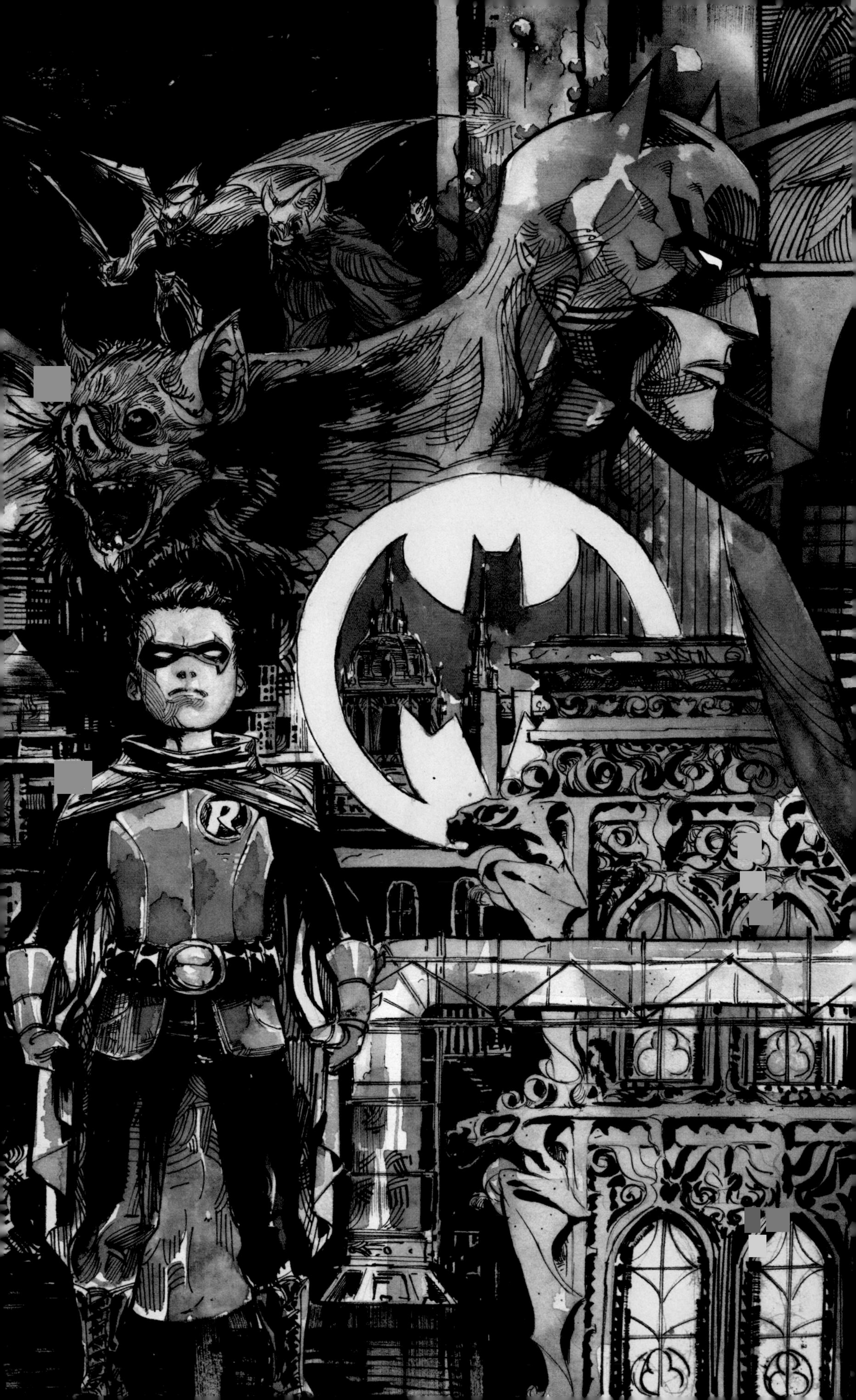

GOTHAM CITY.
WHA--?
He was not what I expected. Heavier. Older.
SMACK
GO AHEAD! BE A HERO!
THAT'S A POLYMER FRAME, VERY RELIABLE, AND WON'T JAM, SO LADY LUCK AIN'T GONNA SAVE YOU.
REMOVE THE WALLET, ROMEO.
His movements were labored. Clumsy.

TAKE THE MONEY--JUST DON'T SHOOT--

HOW MUCH DID THE TRAMP RUN YA?
GO TO HELL--

WHACK

STUPIDEST MISTAKE YOU'D EVER MAKE--

--MR. ANGEL.
LOOKS LIKE YOU GOT THE WHOLE NORMAN ROCKWELL PACKAGE. CUTE KID. BEAUTIFUL WIFE. WONDER HOW SHE'D FEEL IF SHE LEARNED YOU WERE OUT CAROUSING WITH WHORES.
GOTHAM CITY
YOU *ANIMAL!*

YOU WANNA--
A second was all I needed to land a flying knee.
The cartilage in his nose shifted.
CRACK

BOOM
Everything else was just going through the motions.

It ended quickly.

YOU LIKE SLAPPING WOMEN AROUND?

It was a rhetorical question.

YOUR LIP--
IT'S OKAY.

YOU RECOGNIZE THIS GUY, SOPHIA?

SOPHIA?

WAS THAT A GUNSHOT? IS EVERYONE OKAY?

MISS SOPHIA--
EVERYTHING OKAY?
N-NOT REALLY, ANTHONY.

The police were delighted with their unexpected greeting.

HELLO? SOMEONE THERE?

YOU GONNA PLAY GAMES, SAL? 'CAUSE I GOT ALL THE TIME IN THE WORLD. SEE, I CAN GO HOME, TAKE A SHOWER, PUT ON SPORTSCENTER, AND YOU'LL STILL BE HERE.
CAN I *GET* SOME MEDICAL ATTENTION 'FORE I GO BLIND?
YOU AREN'T GETTING ANYTHING 'TIL WE HAVE OURSELVES A REAL DIALOGUE.
WHY'S *HE* HERE, GORDON? TO PUT THE CLAMPS ON ME--
DON'T WORRY 'BOUT HIM. WORRY ABOUT ME.
I AIN'T SAYING ANYTHING 'TIL MY LAWYER--
THESE ARE THE GLOVES YOU WERE WEARING.
I'M NOT TALKING TO HIM--
HEAVILY PADDED.
THIS IS BULL CRAP--
THE FRONT DOOR WAS UNLOCKED. THERE WERE BLANKS IN THE GUN. THE GIRL CHEWED BLOOD TABLETS--
NO ONE READ ME MY MIRANDA RIGHTS--
BAM
THINK I'LL GET A DRINK OF WATER AND LEAVE YOU TWO ALONE.
TAKE YOUR TIME. GRAB YOURSELF A DANISH.
*NO.* NO. STAY...

OH GOD, OH GOD-- I DIDN'T WANT TO DO IT...I NEEDED THE MONEY--WE ONLY DID IT A COUPLE TIMES--IT WASN'T LIKE THESE GUYS WERE UPSTANDING CITIZENS OR ANYTHING-- I'M SO SORRY--I DON'T WANNA GO TO JAIL--
YOU WERE BLACKMAILING THESE MEN, SOPHIA?
YEAH. SAL WOULD SCARE THE CRAP OUTTA THEM.
TAKE SOME SUGGESTIVE PICTURES AND THREATEN TO SEND THEM TO THEIR WIVES, GIRLFRIENDS.
IF THEY BALKED HE'D JUST ROLL THEM FOR THEIR MONEY. CREDIT CARDS. WATCHES. WHATEVER HE COULD GET.
OH GOD! HOW LONG--
DO ANY OF THESE MEN LOOK FAMILIAR TO YOU?
OH MY...
...WHY'RE YOU SHOWING ME THESE?

BECAUSE YOU KILLED THEM.
I DID NOT! YOU TAKE THAT BACK! I DIDN'T KILL ANYONE!
THEN WHO DID, SOPHIA? BECAUSE OUR WORLD'S TURNING INTO A REAL GORDIAN KNOT AND YOU AREN'T GETTING OUT EASY.
IF I WERE A JURY, I SURE AS HELL WOULDN'T TAKE YOUR WORD, NO MATTER HOW MANY BIBLES YOU SWORE ON.
I DID NOT KILL ANYONE--
CUT THE CRAP AND GIVE ME A NAME.
I DIDN'T--
A NAME!
...
ROLAND. ROLAND DAVIS.

WHO IS HE TO YOU?
EX-BOYFRIEND.
HE USED TO BOUNCE AT THE CLUB 'TIL HE GOT FIRED FOR BEING A PSYCHOPATH. STUPID 'ROID HEAD. I DON'T OWE HIM ANYTHING--
WHY'D HE GET FIRED?
BECAUSE HE'S CUCKOO. ONE NIGHT SOME HEDGE FUND JERK STARTS PLAYING GRAB ASS--NO BIG DEAL--HAPPENS EVERY NIGHT.
ONLY ROLAND GETS ALL JEALOUS AN LEAPS ON TOP OF THE POOR SAP--NEARLY BEA HIM TO DEATH. TOOK FI BOUNCERS TO RESTRA HIM. NOT SOMEONE I WA SHARE MY BED WITH.
WHEN DID YOU SEE HIM LAST?
THIS EVENING. HE WAS OUTSIDE THE CLUB, WAITING FOR ME. HE STARTED WITH THAT GUY I WAS WITH--JAMES...
DAMMIT. I HAD THE GUY.
SO YOU BELIEVE HER?
FOR WHATEVER REASON, I DO.
AND THE OTHER ONE--SAL?
HE'S NOT OUR MAN.
BUT RELEASE THE GIRL.
EXCUSE ME?
LET HER GO.
I HEARD YOU. LOOK, BATMAN, EVEN IF SHE DIDN'T HAVE ANYTHING TO DO WITH THESE MURDERS--WHICH I'M NOT ENTIRELY CONVINCED OF--SHE'S AN ACCOMPLICE TO ARMED ROBBERY.
UNDERSTOOD. BUT THERE'S A BIGG PLAY TO BE MADE. I ASKING YOU TO TA A CHANCE.

THANKS, ANTHONY.
YOU OKAY, MISS SOPHIA?
BEEN BETTER.

ANYTHING I CAN DO--JUST ASK.

LATER THAT NIGHT...

WE TOOK A HELICOPTER TO HIS PRIVATE YACHT. THIS THING WAS GIGANTIC. YOU COULD LIKE *LIVE* ON IT.

THAT'S WHERE I MET THE SULTAN.

I'LL MAKE AN INTRODUCTION. HE'S COMING BACK TO GOTHAM NEXT MONTH.

YOU'D LOVE HIM. HE'S ACTUALLY PRETTY FUNNY.
ROLAND?

YOU ALL RIGHT, GIRL?
YEAH, THOUGHT I SAW SOMEBODY. I'M NOT FEELING SO WELL.
THEN GO HOME AND GET SOME REST. NO ONE GOOD HERE TONIGHT ANYWAY.

HEY, WHAT ARE YOU--
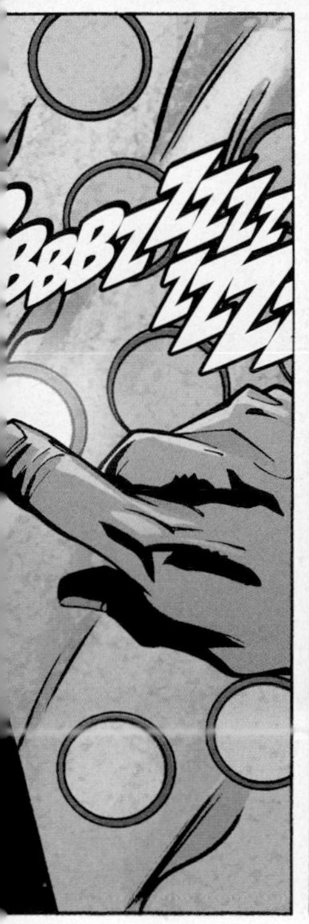
BBBZZZZZ ZZZZZ

*STOP.* I'M NOT GOING TO HURT YOU. BUT YOU CAN'T SCREAM, OKAY? DO YOU UNDERSTAND?

WHAT DO YOU WANT FROM ME, ROLAND?
JUST HEAR ME OUT AND I'LL GO--

BABY, LOOK, THINGS GOT ALL TWISTED UP--I NEVER MEANT FOR ANY OF THIS TO HAPPEN. EVERY TIME I SEE YOU--ALL I WANT IS FOR THINGS TO GO BACK TO HOW THEY WERE.
I WANNA TAKE CARE OF YOU, SOPHIA. I KNOW I SCREWED UP--
PLEASE, GO...

I LOVE YOU. I'LL DO WHATEVER I NEED TO GET YOU BACK.

ROLAND--I CAN'T DO THIS ANYMORE. MAYBE IF YOU GAVE ME SOME TIME TO PUT THINGS IN PERSPECTIVE...

FINE. YEAH. TAKE YOUR TIME. BUT PROMISE ME YOU'LL--

WHACK

ANTHONY!

CRACK
AHHHHHH!

STUPID TRAMP!

DO NOT MOVE!

YOU WERE SPOTTED AT THE CLUB THE NIGHT OF EACH MURDER.
WHY YOU KEEP SAYING THAT?

I'M TELLING YOU THE TRUTH.
SO YOU SAY.

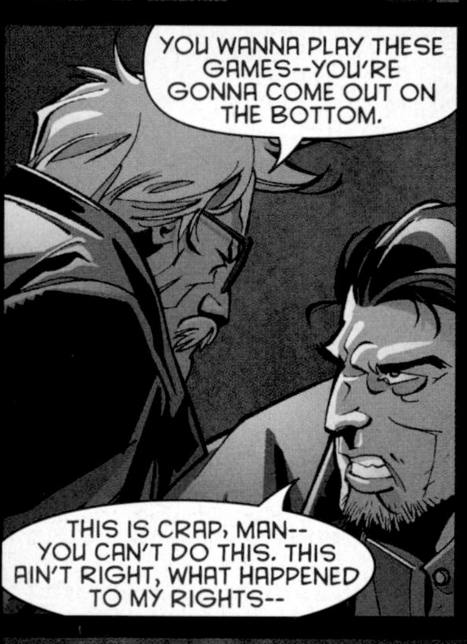
YOU WANNA PLAY THESE GAMES--YOU'RE GONNA COME OUT ON THE BOTTOM.
THIS IS CRAP, MAN-- YOU CAN'T DO THIS. THIS AIN'T RIGHT, WHAT HAPPENED TO MY RIGHTS--

YOU LOST THEM WHEN YOU STARTED KILLING PEOPLE.

YOU COULDN'T STAND SEEING SOPHIA WITH OTHER MEN. YOU STARTED UP WITH EACH OF THEM--
GOT ANY HARD EVIDENCE-- ANY OF MY BLOOD? I MAY HAVE SLAPPED HER BUT I DIDN'T KIL ANYONE, FREAK.

YOU KILLED THOSE MEN.
WHAPP

THAT'LL BE ENOUGH, BATMAN.

SO WHATDYA THINK?
NOT SURE YET.
ALIBIS ALL CHECKED OUT. I CAN'T HOLD HIM MUCH LONGER, LET ALONE HERE.
YOU KNOW AS WELL AS I DO, IF HE DID THIS--FIRST THING HE DOES IS PAY OUR GIRL A VISIT.
YOU HAVE AN IDEA?
I DO, BUT YOU'RE NOT GOING TO LIKE IT.
TRY ME.

Batman was right. I didn't like it.
I THINK I LIKE YOUR MASK BETTER THAN MINE.
AS LONG AS THE PROSTHETICS STAY ON, I'LL BE HAPPY. YOU ABOUT READY?
WE BEEN HERE LONG ENOUGH?
I THINK SO.

THEN LETS GO.

We paraded across the floor, out in the open. If someone were looking, they'd have a hard time **not** spotting us.

STUPID TRAMP.

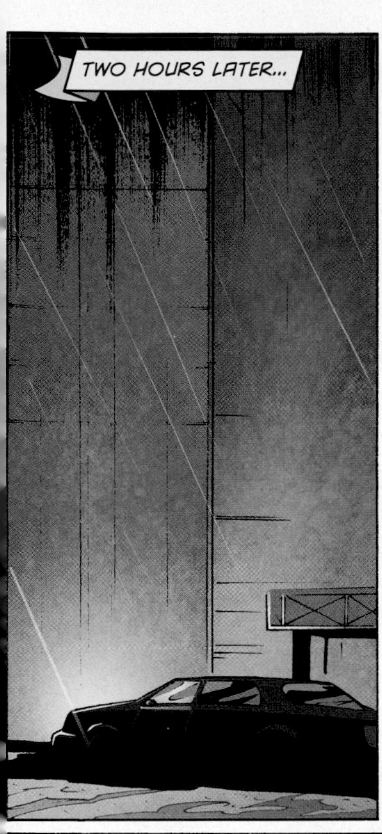
TWO HOURS LATER...

SIR?
ARE YOU OKAY?
WHAT--?
ROLAND?
SO HOW *WAS* SHE? YOU HAVE FUN WITH HER LIKE THE OTHERS? HUH?

YOU DIDN'T ANSWER MY QUESTION.
DON'T COME ANY CLOSER.
LET ME SEE YOUR HANDS.

This was more what I was expecting. Big. **Brutal.**
Mad. But size doesn't matter when the windpipe is struck just so. Even the **mightiest** fall.
LET'S TRY THIS AGAIN. MOVE AND YOU DIE!
THIS WHOLE TIME...IT WAS ANTHONY...MY DOORMAN...
IT'S OVER NOW, SOPHIA.

A second chance. A do-over.
YOU DIDN'T HAVE TO DO THIS, YOU KNOW.
MY GOOD DEED FOR THE DAY.
I STILL CAN'T BELIEVE IT WAS ANTHONY. HE WORKED IN MY BUILDING FOREVER.
WELL, NOW HE'LL BE WORKING A CELL FOR THE REST OF HIS LIFE.
Not everybody gets one...
TAKE CARE OF YOURSELF, SOPHIA.
WOULD YOU THANK *HIM* FOR ME?
WILL DO.
...but sometimes opportunity has a funny way of favoring those who've paid the price.
END

"THE ARENA'S A HIT, MR. ZSASZ. SELL-OUT CROWDS EVERY NIGHT SINCE DECEMBER..."

...THERE'S EVEN A WAITING LIST A MONTH LONG.

NEVER UNDERESTIMATE THE BASENESS OF HUMAN ANIMALS, BUDDY. PROMISE THEM A MURDER AND THEY'LL PAY A FORTUNE TO SEE IT.

RIGHT, SIR. BUT WE'RE RUNNING INTO A PROBLEM.
I DON'T KEEP YOU *ALIVE* TO CREATE PROBLEMS FOR ME, BUDDY.
N-NO, SIR. BUT OUR GUYS ON THE STREET SAY IT'S GETTING HARDER TO FIND KIDS.
NOT MY PROBLEM, BUDDY. *YOURS.*
I'LL HAVE A FULL CARD TONIGHT, OR YOU'RE FACING ME IN THE ARENA. OPENING BOUT.
DON'T WORRY, BOSS. I'M ON IT.

Ever since I can remember, it's always been about Heroes.
THE HEROES

Even at the very beginning, in the orphanage.

My first memory was of old George showing me their pictures.

They were strong. They were powerful.

And better than that, they were **good.**
BATMAN !

I never really expected to be swept into that world, but all that changed when the villain Scarecrow kidnapped me in a plot to kill Batman.

He strapped me down and pumped me full of this stuff, Venom. It's what they used to create the villain Bane.

It hurt pretty bad.

I was in pain and lashed out at my hero.

Then I went after Scarecrow. I was angry and wanted to beat him to death. Batman wouldn't let me. He stopped me from becoming a killer.

For the first time in my life, I knew what it was like to have someone care about me.

And even though Batman said I'd be okay, the Venom never left my body, not all of it.

And if I concentrated really hard...

...I could control it.
I knew I'd never be like Flash or Green Lantern. Not one of the friendly-looking heroes people are happy to see.

But even if I looked like a **monster,** I could still act like a **hero.**

I started with some thugs who used to prey on us orphans. They knew we didn't have any money, they just beat us up for the fun of it.

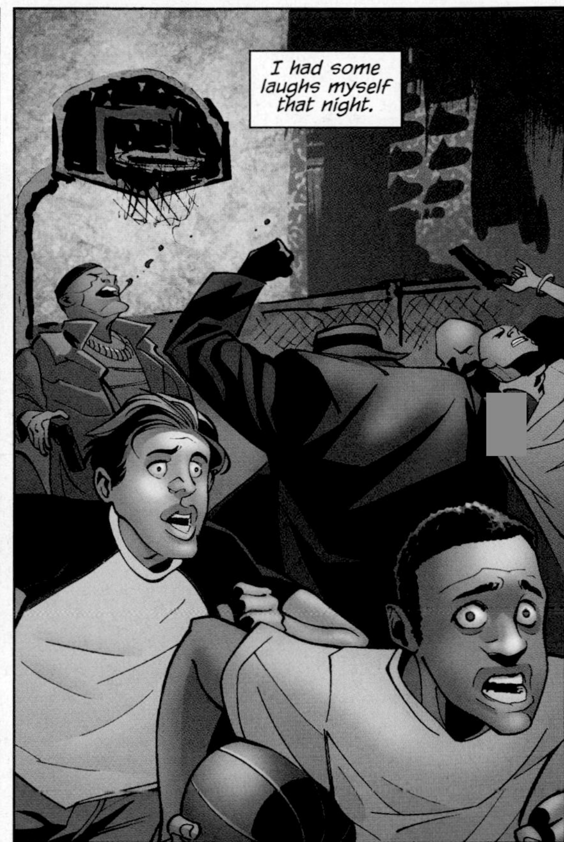
I had some laughs myself that night.

Sister Agnes taught me stealing is a **sin.**

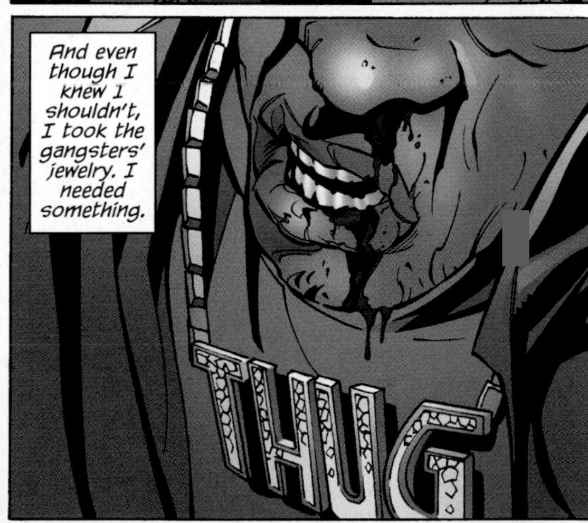
And even though I knew I shouldn't, I took the gangsters' jewelry. I needed something.
THUG

I cashed it in at a pawn shop and took the money to someone I'd heard about, someone I wasn't sure even existed. After a few days, I finally found her.
I'M LOOKING FOR JONESY. I WANT TO BUY SOMETHING.
THIS AIN'T WAL-MART. GET LOST.

CRUNNCH

I HEAR YOU MAKE THINGS. DOESN'T MATTER WHICH SIDE YOU'RE ON, IF A BUYER MEETS YOUR PRICE, YOU'LL GIVE THEM WHAT THEY WANT.
FOR YOU IT'LL BE MORE. MY CARPENTER WILL HAVE TO REDO THAT DOOR, AND THE GIRL I USE AIN'T CHEAP.
I WANT TWO OF THESE.
ABUSE
UH-HUH. GOLD OR BRASS?
WHICH WOULD HURT MORE WHEN SLUGGED INTO A FACE?
BRASS.
THEN BRASS.
Jonesy never asked what I wanted the knuckles for. She never asks anyone what they do with the stuff she makes for them...
...but three weeks later they were ready and I was in business.
ABUSE
ABUSE

I wanted to protect kids like me who had been given a crap deal in life.
Turn some of that suffering back on the creeps who abused kids, with a way of letting the world know what they did.
ABUSE
Batman rescues Janitor from flaming building!
Fredo's Pasta House destroyed.
DANGEROUS NEW VIGILANTE STALKS GOTHAM!
So far it's been pretty sweet. No one knows the monster tearing through Gotham's dirtbags is a kid.
MONST
TARGETS
UNDERWO
"ABUSE" HERO OR MENACE?
After all, who would think to look for him in an orphanage?
Even Batman doesn't suspect the helpless kid he rescued is fast becoming his greatest ally.
Maybe someday it will be Batman, Robin and ME.
Wow. That would be cool.

'Course, for that to happen, I'd have to prove myself on a major scale, like bringing down the psycho who's been killing runaway kids.
My first lead was Christmas Eve, when I encountered **Humpty Dumpty.**
I thought he might be the killer, but it turned out Humpty had found the kids' bodies and was trying to "fix" them.
I can't forget the look on Robin's face when he saw the bodies.
I'LL GET THE MONSTER THAT DID THIS!
**WE'LL** GET HIM.
I overheard Humpty say he had found the bodies in the river.
Now that the ice is finally melting, I might pick up a few clues.
I know I'm in for a shouting match with Grayson when he finds me gone.
**Let** him shout. Two months we've played it his way.

Shaking down squealers and low-level thugs at night--nothing. None of them knew anything, and why would they?
They're common crooks. I'm after an **animal.** Only way to stalk it is in its own territory.
And, if in the process, the monster mistakes me for a target, then I've got him.
HELLO.
HEY, KID. IT'S NOT SAFE TO WANDER AROUND THIS AREA ALONE.
I COULD SAY THE SAME THING TO YOU.
THE DIFFERENCE IS I KNOW WHAT I'M DOING.
YEAH, WELL, I CAN LOOK OUT FOR MYSELF, TOO.
I LOST SOME FRIENDS AROUND HERE. AT LEAST, THIS WAS WHERE THEIR *BODIES* WASHED UP.

I HEARD WHAT HAPPENED TO THEM ***BEFORE*** THEY HIT THE WATER MUST HAVE BEEN HORRIBLE.

I GOT A LOOK AT THE BODIES. UP CLOSE.

"THE VICTIMS WERE STABBED REPEATEDLY IN THE FACE AND TORSO.

"SMALL CUTS, WITHOUT MUCH STRENGTH BEHIND THEM. MOST OF THE KIDS LOOKED LIKE THEY DIED OF BLOOD LOSS."

BUT A FEW BODIES HAD OTHER CUTS ON THEM--BIG, BROAD STROKES, DONE WITH ALMOST ***SURGICAL*** ACCURACY.

WHOA. HOW'D YOU SEE ALL ***THAT?*** IS YOUR DAD A COP?

SOMETHING LIKE THAT.
MY NAME'S DAMIAN.
I'M COLIN.

AND YOU CAN CALL ME ***BUDDY.***

HEY, COLIN. HEY, DAMIAN. ISN'T THIS AWESOME? WE JUST MET AND ALREADY WE'RE FRIENDS.
Don't trust this creep.
He tries anything and he's dead.

YOU GUYS LOOK COLD AND HUNGRY. YOU WANNA EAT? IT DON'T COST NOTHING.
GET OUT OF HERE.
RUN. DO IT.

MY FRIENDS WILL SHOW YOU THE WAY.

HURRY UP! ZSASZ NEEDS THEM NOW!
Zsasz. The worst of them all.
Zsasz. Of course.

DON'T BE SCARED.
I'M NOT.

INSIDE, MEAT!
UNNGH!
Go along with it. Pretend to be scared. Wait until they're off guard, **then** change!
NOW YOU!
TOUCH ME AGAIN AND I'LL BREAK YOUR ARM.
YEAH, GO ON, SMARTASS!
ROBIN! Has to be!
SNAP
AUGHH!

GRAB HIM!
I need a weapon.

AAHHH!
The broken-armed dirtbag works fine.

HEY! WHAT THE HELL...?!

JEEZUS!

MR. ZSASZ!
MAKE THIS IMPORTANT, BUDDY.

COME ON! GET OUT OF HERE!
I'M STAYING! I CAN HELP YOU!

YOU WANT TO HELP? FIND A PHONE AND CALL GORDON! TELL HIM TO BRING A SWAT TEAM!
NO! YOU DON'T UNDERSTAND! I KNOW WHO YOU ARE!

ROBIN, WE CAN BRING DOWN ZSASZ TOGETHER! YOU'VE GOT TO TRUST ME!
OH, DAMN IT...

I'LL SHOW Y--
THUDD

SORRY, KID, YOU'RE OUT OF YOUR LEAGUE!

ZSASZ!
How could my father allow a creature like Zsasz to live?! Was it weakness that always stayed his hand, or guilt?
More likely a foolish belief that brute could be helped back to "sanity."
ANSWER ME, MONSTER!
There's only one sure way to fix Zsasz's head--remove it.
ZSASZ!

Perhaps I should have let him come to me.

USUALLY A BOY HAS TO WIN SEVERAL PRELIMINARY ROUNDS BEFORE HE GETS TO ME.

BUT WHEN BUDDY TOLD ME WE HAD SUCH AN ENTHUSIASTIC PLAYER, I JUST HAD TO OBLIGE HIM.

YOU'RE DEAD, YOU SICK BASTARD.

SHUT UP AND FIGHT, CORPSE.

Missed?! Impossible!

Wait, my shoulder...
I'm bleeding. But he was nowhere near...
AGH!
No. This does not happen.
I was trained by the League of Assassins. I know a hundred ways to kill a man.
Zsasz moves without pattern or strategy, yet somehow becomes a living part of the knife!

No...!

The crowd roars, my side screams...

Focus, damn it! Fight through...

GAME OVER, DEAD KID.

I hurry as fast as I can toward the bloodthirsty crowd. I don't want to miss the show.

FINAL CUT
Zsasz's last show. I swear it.

LEAVE HIM ALONE!
HA! YOU TELL HIM, KID!
The monsters scream and throw trash. Fine.
In a minute they'll have something else to scream about.
A BONUS MATCH. I LOVE IT.

A SMALL DIVERSION BEFORE THE MAIN KILL.
COLIN...
RUN.
STUPID KID...!
YES, RUN, LITTLE PIG. RUN AND CRY. MAKE IT FUN FOR ME.
I SAID RUN!
NO.

WHAT THE HELL ARE YOU?!
SURPRISE.
LET GO!
NOT A CHANCE.
AGHH!
HAVING FUN YET?

ME? I'M HAVING A BLAST!
AAAGH!

WHO THE HELL IS THAT FREAK?!
YOU ASK HIM! I'M GONE!

STICK AROUND. THE PARTY'S JUST GETTING STARTED!

Zsasz... where...?
Unconscious. Dead, if we're lucky. Totally underestimated him. He may be mortal, but he's hardly human.
Wrote off that Colin kid, too. Never dreamed he was someone like me.
Another mistake because I rushed in without thinking. Didn't even bring my mask and costume, either.
This will do.
WAIT! I NEVER HURT NO ONE!
YOU'RE ONE UP ON ME, MAN.
Anyone who pays for the "pleasure" of watching kids kill each other deserves everything I can deliver.
And even then, it's not enough.

The sisters try to teach us a lot of Bible lessons at St. Aidan's. Lots of "turn the other cheek" and Noah's Ark. It's boring. They sugarcoat the rougher stuff.

But one time Sister Agnes told me the story of Cain and Abel.
Cain murdered his own brother in cold blood.

BANG
When the Lord found out what Cain had done, He exiled Cain from the Garden of Eden.

And He marked Cain. This meant no one would harm him--but they would all know what he'd done, and he'd have to live with that.

Most of the other kids thought God should have just killed Cain and been done with it.

I figure if it works for God, it works for me.

C'MON! RUSH HIM!

THANKS.

PLEASUR--
HEY!

SMASH
OH...

WHY DIDN'T YOU TELL ME YOU WERE ALL... Y'KNOW?
TRIED. YOU KNOCKED ME OUT.

SO TALK FASTER NEXT TIME.

I was supposed to see a local jazz guitarist tonight. No big deal, just something to remind myself I'm not Bruce.
WE CAN'T JUST BOLT! ZSASZ WILL KILL US!
Unfortunately, Damian went AWOL, so the long overdue night off is--yet again--postponed.
I'D SAY THE MONSTER KID SOLVED THAT PROBLEM FOR US. KEEP GOIN'!
Fortunately, Damian's cycle has a tracking beacon.
EVENING.
WHO...?
So here I am, in front of a slaughterhouse with two terrified thugs. Whatever's happening inside can't be good.
AW, HELL.
I'M GOING TO ASK THIS ONCE...
IT WASN'T US, MAN! IT WAS ZSASZ! HE'S INSANE! HE MADE US TAKE THOSE KIDS!

Kids. The orphans Humpty Dumpty found murdered in the river.
WHERE ARE...
THEY'RE IN THERE!

SO'S ZSASZ! YOU CAN STILL GET HIM! JUST DON'T HURT US!
Guess I'm more like Bruce than I thought.

The henchmen bolt away, figuring I'll cut them a break for fingering their boss. I am grateful...

POOM

...to a point.

I'm bleeding...
I GOT YA, MR. ZSASZ. IT'S ME--BUDDY.

BUDDY, YES.
MY HAND IS BROKEN...
STAY WITH ME. I'LL GET YOU OUT OF HERE.

THAT THING, THAT MONSTER! HE'S RUINED ME!

I'll see him dead for this, him and that other kid!

I'LL DANCE IN THEIR BLOOD...
BOSS! YOU DON'T STAND A CHANCE! HE'S A FREAK!

NO. I'VE SEEN WHAT HE IS.
UIK...

UNDERNEATH THAT MUSCLE, HE'S JUST A *KID.*

ALL HIS POTENTIAL, ALL HIS POWER WASTED IN THROWING TANTRUMS. I'M GOING TO TAKE IT FROM HIM.

THE BEST KILL OF MY CAREER.

FIVE HATCH MARKS FOR HIM ALONE.

THAT'S THE PROBLEM WITH YOU KIDS--ALWAYS TRYING TO GROW UP TOO FAST!
AHH!

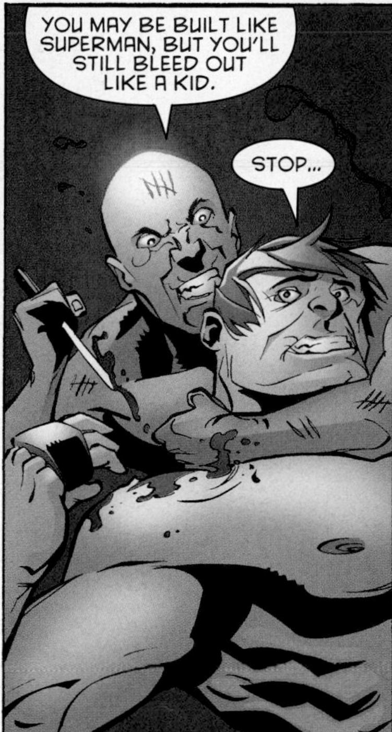
YOU MAY BE BUILT LIKE SUPERMAN, BUT YOU'LL STILL BLEED OUT LIKE A KID.
STOP...

THAT'S ALL YOU ARE, A KID. SCARED, WHIMPERING...

...ALONE.

DID YOU FORGET ABOUT *ME?*

YOU OKAY?
I'LL LIVE.

TWO OF US WILL.
WAIT, DON'T...
DON'T KILL HIM. JUST, I DON'T KNOW, STOP HIM SOMEHOW.
AFTER WHAT HE'S DONE?!
BATMAN COULD HAVE KILLED ME ONCE... BUT HE DIDN'T. THAT'S WHAT MAKES HIM A HERO.
HUH. YOU REALLY ARE A KID IN THERE, AREN'T YOU?

FUNNY. A MASK IS SUPPOSED TO BE A DISGUISE. NOW THAT YOU'VE HIDDEN YOUR FACE, I KNOW WHO YOU REALLY ARE.
AND I KNOW HOW THE BAT WILL ***AGONIZE*** WHEN HE SEES WHAT I'VE DONE TO YOU.
*My mistake was thinking Zsasz would fight on my level.*
*So I'll shut out sanity and fight on his.*
*This is wrong...*
*I see the world in shades of red, everyone my victim. Suddenly this one isn't a corpse to me any longer.*
*No...*

HUH... THE LAST HATCH MARK.

I ALWAYS THOUGHT I'D SAVE IT FOR ME. A FINAL STAB AT REPENTANCE...

THERE. YOU'RE WELCOME.
WHAT DO YOU MEAN?
I SPARED THE ANIMAL, AS YOU INSISTED. ZSASZ HIMSELF MAY BELIEVE HE'S DEAD, BUT I PULLED MY STROKE AT THE LAST SECOND, JUST SHORT OF SEVERING HIS SPINE.
THEN ROBIN'S REPUTATION MEANS SOMETHING TO YOU AFTER ALL.
THIS MAY SHOCK THE NAIVE LITTLE BOY INSIDE YOU, COLIN, BUT I'M NOT LOOKING TO PLAY ROBIN FOR THE REST OF MY LIFE.
PERSONALLY, I DON'T GIVE A DAMN ABOUT...
WHERE IS ZSASZ?
IN THE PIT, IF HE HASN'T ALREADY BEEN WASHED INTO THE RIVER. HE MAY NEED A BAND-AID.
DID YOU KILL HIM?
WHAT DO WE LOOK LIKE, HOMICIDAL MANIACS?
HE BROUGHT IT ON HIMSELF. WE JUST DEFENDED OURSELVES.

IS THAT WHAT HAPPENED?
THAT'S WHAT HAPPENED.
THE END